50

# GREAT GIFTS

Gillian Souter

**Gareth Stevens Publishing**
A WORLD ALMANAC EDUCATION GROUP COMPANY

# ✷ Before You Start ✷

Some of these projects can get messy, so make sure your work area is covered with newspaper. For projects that need paint, you can use acrylic paint, poster paint, or any other kind of paint that is labeled nontoxic. Ask an adult to help you find a paint that is safe to use. You will need an adult's help with some projects, especially when you have to stitch material, use a craft knife, or bake something in the oven.

Please visit our web site at: **www.garethstevens.com**
**For a free color catalog describing Gareth Stevens' list of high-quality books and multimedia programs, call 1-800-542-2595 (USA) or 1-800-461-9120 (Canada). Gareth Stevens Publishing's Fax: (414) 332-3567.**

Souter, Gillian
    Great Gifts / by Gillian Souter
      p. cm. -- (Handy crafts)
    Includes bibliographical references and index.
    ISBN 0-8368-2820-8 (lib. bdg.)
    1. Handicraft--Juvenile literature.  2. Gifts--Juvenile literature.
    [1. Handicraft.  2. Gifts.]  I. Title  II. Series.
    TT157 .S36796   2001
    745.5--dc21                  00-052242

This U.S. edition first published in 2001 by
**Gareth Stevens Publishing**
A World Almanac Education Group Company
330 West Olive Street, Suite 100
Milwaukee, Wisconsin 53212 USA

This U.S. edition © 2001 by Gareth Stevens, Inc. Original edition published as *Great Gifts* in 1999 by Off the Shelf Publishing, 32 Thomas Street, Lewisham NSW 2049, Australia. Text, projects, and layout © 1999 by Off the Shelf Publishing. Additional end matter © 2001 by Gareth Stevens, Inc.

Line illustrations: Clare Watson
Photographs: Andre Martin
Cover design: Joel Bucaro
Gareth Stevens editor: Monica Rausch

Printed in the United States of America

1 2 3 4 5 6 7 8 9 05 04 03 02 01

# Contents

Crafty Cards . . . . . . . . . . . . . . . 4

Magic Rocks . . . . . . . . . . . . . 6

Brilliant Badges . . . . . . . . . . . 8

Rainbow Rings . . . . . . . . . . . 10

Perrrfect Purrrse . . . . . . . . . 12

Letter Box . . . . . . . . . . . . . . 14

Shmoos . . . . . . . . . . . . . . 16

Mug Mats . . . . . . . . . . . . . 18

Swish Dish . . . . . . . . . . . . 20

Pencil Pouch . . . . . . . . . . . . 22

Hot Pot Hot Pad . . . . . . . . 24

Mark My Words . . . . . . . . . . . 26

Bloomers . . . . . . . . . . . . . . . 28

Take Note! . . . . . . . . . . . . . 30

A Frame-up . . . . . . . . . . . . . 32

String Thing . . . . . . . . . . . . 34

Stick 'Em Up . . . . . . . . . . . 36

Mouse Madness. . . . . . . . . . 38

Bath Buddy . . . . . . . . . . . . 40

Killer Key Rings . . . . . . . . . 42

Foxy Boxes . . . . . . . . . . . 44

It's a Wrap! . . . . . . . . . . . . 46

Glossary . . . . . . . . . . . . . . 48

More Craft Books . . . . . . . . . 48

Index . . . . . . . . . . . . . . . 48

# Crafty Cards

**Cards can be great gifts just by themselves. Check out these ideas for making creative cards.**

To make a card, fold a rectangle of thin cardboard in half. Ask an adult to run a craft knife lightly across the inside of the fold to make the fold sharper.

You can add all kinds of decorations to your card. This card has felt shapes held on with a paper fastener.

Tags tell us who is giving a present — and who is getting it! Use a hole punch to make a hole in a tag. Then pull ribbon through the hole and tie the ribbon to the present.

Try using colored paper to decorate a card. Tear the paper into pieces. Arrange the torn pieces on the card to make a fun design, then glue the pieces in place.

For a friend's birthday, you can make an "age" card. With a pencil, draw your friend's age on a card. Roll small squares of tissue paper into balls and glue them over the pencil lines.

5

# Magic Rocks

**A pretty rock makes a perfect paperweight, and the shiny designs add a little magic to anyone's desk.**

1 Paint the rocks white. When the paint is dry, paint each rock a bright color, such as purple, blue, or red.

2 On a purple rock, draw little swirls with a silver or gold pen. Brush on a coat of clear varnish.

3 On a blue rock, brush on clear varnish first. When the varnish is dry, stick silver or gold stars all over the rock. You may need to use glue to help the stars stick.

4 On a red rock, brush on varnish and let it dry. Place a zigzag of white glue on the top of the rock, then sprinkle glitter over the glue. When the glue is dry, shake off any extra glitter.

**★ Bright Idea ★**
Try gluing on pieces of aluminum foil or colored paper to decorate your rocks.

7

# Brilliant Badges

**You can have loads of fun with papier-mâché — and create beautiful badges.**

### You Will Need

- pencil
- cardboard
- scissors
- white glue
- bowl
- newspaper
- paintbrush
- acrylic paints
- clear varnish
- strong tape
- safety pin

**1** Use a pencil to draw a cool shape on cardboard. Cut out the shape of your badge.

**2** Mix equal amounts of white glue and water in a bowl.

**3** Tear newspaper into narrow strips. Dip each strip into the glue mixture and stick it onto the cardboard shape, overlapping the strips as you go. Cover the badge with several layers of strips, then let the badge dry.

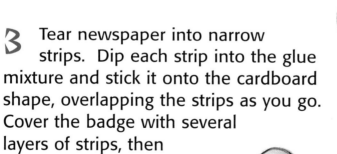

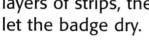

**4** Paint the badge white. When the paint is dry, use a pencil to draw a design on the badge.

**5** Now paint your design bright colors. Let each color of paint dry before you paint another color. When the last color of paint is dry, brush on clear varnish.

**6** Let the varnish dry, then use strong tape to tape a large safety pin on the back of the badge.

**★ Helpful Hint ★**
Tape the unmovable bar of the safety pin to the badge, so you can open the pin.

# Rainbow Rings

**With these colorful napkin rings, you can have a rainbow at your table.**

## You Will Need

- ruler and pencil
- cardboard tube
- craft knife
- paintbrush
- white paint
- double-sided tape
- embroidery floss
- clear tape
- scissors and needle

1 Draw a line around a thick cardboard tube 1 ½ inches (4 centimeters) from the end. Ask an adult to carefully cut along the line with a craft knife.

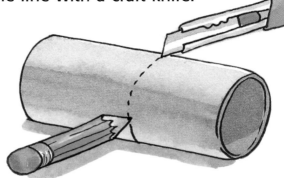

2 Now you have a cardboard ring. Paint the ring white. When the paint is dry, tape a strip of double-sided tape around the outside of the ring.

★ **Bright Idea** ★
Cut narrow rings out of
a wide cardboard tube and
make rainbow bracelets.

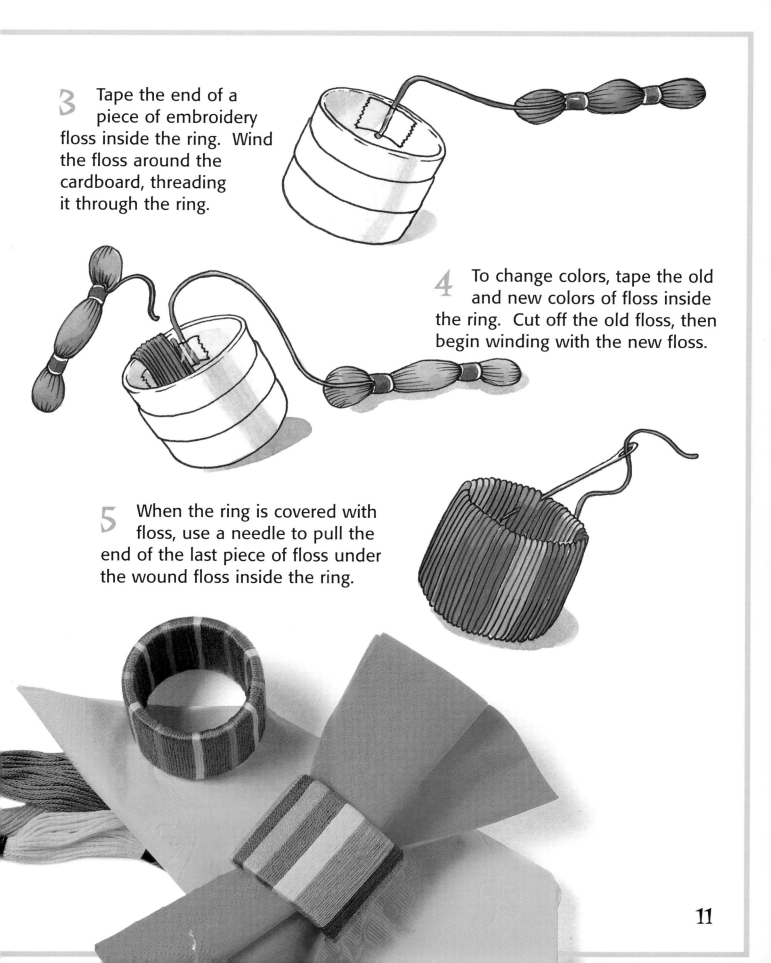

3 Tape the end of a piece of embroidery floss inside the ring. Wind the floss around the cardboard, threading it through the ring.

4 To change colors, tape the old and new colors of floss inside the ring. Cut off the old floss, then begin winding with the new floss.

5 When the ring is covered with floss, use a needle to pull the end of the last piece of floss under the wound floss inside the ring.

# Perrrfect Purrrse

**This fancy felt purse can hold a friend's treasures.**

1 Cut a piece of felt 5 inches by 11 inches (13 cm by 28 cm). Fold a short side over 4 inches (10 cm) to make a pocket, then pin the sides together.

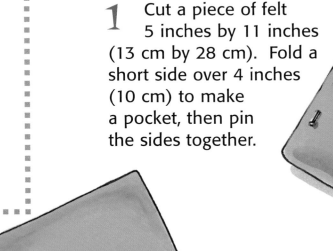

2 With a needle and thread, sew together each side of the pocket in small, neat stitches. You might need to ask an adult to help you with the sewing.

3 Use a glass or a lid and a pencil to draw curves at the corners of the pocket's flap. Cut along the curves.

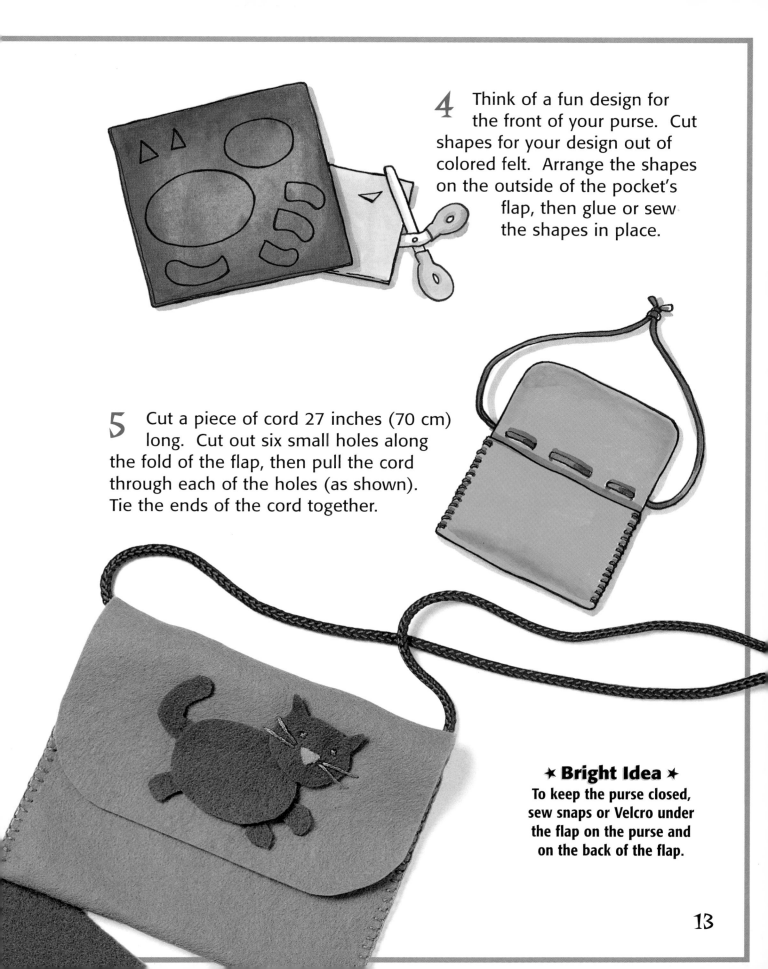

**4** Think of a fun design for the front of your purse. Cut shapes for your design out of colored felt. Arrange the shapes on the outside of the pocket's flap, then glue or sew the shapes in place.

**5** Cut a piece of cord 27 inches (70 cm) long. Cut out six small holes along the fold of the flap, then pull the cord through each of the holes (as shown). Tie the ends of the cord together.

★ **Bright Idea** ★
To keep the purse closed, sew snaps or Velcro under the flap on the purse and on the back of the flap.

13

# Letter Box

**Make something new out of old stamps — a marvelous mail holder.**

### You Will Need

- pencil
- ruler
- empty cereal box
- scissors
- cardboard
- white glue
- paintbrush
- black paint
- stamps
- clear varnish

1 Draw a line across the front of a cereal box 4 inches (10 cm) from the box's bottom. On the back of the box, draw a line across the box 6 inches (15 cm) from the bottom.

2 Cut along these lines. Cut the sides of the box on a slant, connecting the lines. Keep the bottom part of the box.

3 To make a divider for the box, cut a piece of cardboard slightly wider than the box and 5 inches (13 cm) high. Fold in a short flap on three sides of the cardboard. Cut out squares at the corners where the flaps overlap. Glue the flaps to the inside of the box.

14

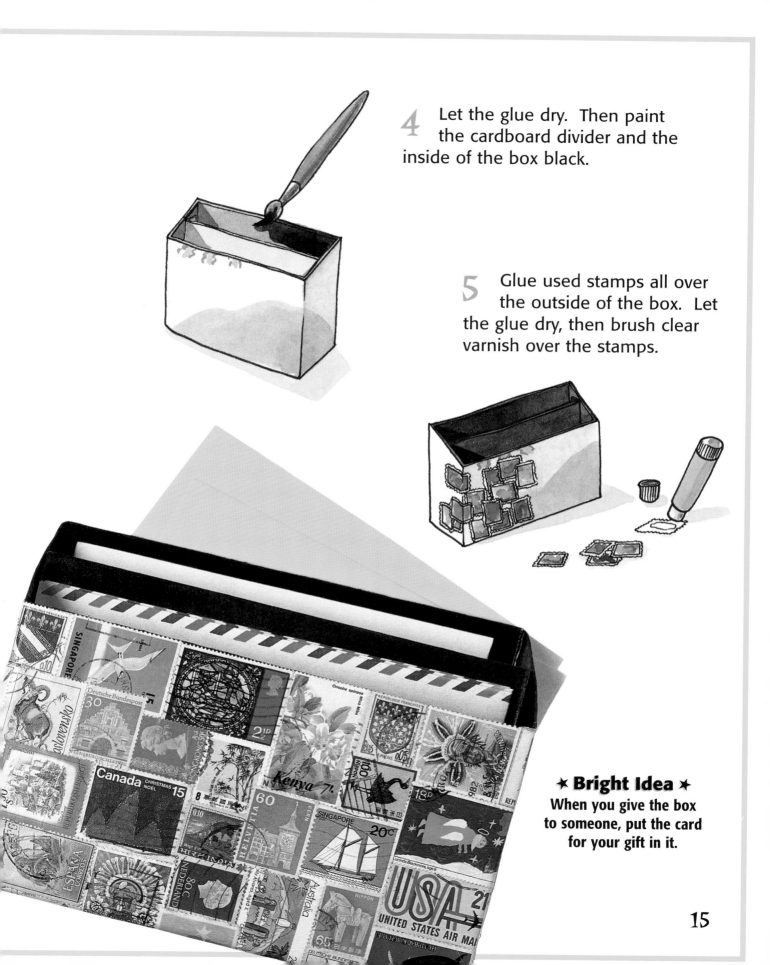

**4** Let the glue dry. Then paint the cardboard divider and the inside of the box black.

**5** Glue used stamps all over the outside of the box. Let the glue dry, then brush clear varnish over the stamps.

**★ Bright Idea ★**
When you give the box to someone, put the card for your gift in it.

15

# Shmoos

**Are any grown-ups you know nervous? They can squoosh this shmoo to stay cool.**

**You Will Need**
- balloon
- funnel
- spoon
- flour
- chopstick
- colored electrical tape
- scissors

1  Stretch a balloon by blowing air into it, then let the air out. Stick the end of the funnel into the balloon's opening, pulling the balloon's neck around the funnel.

2  Spoon some flour into the balloon through the funnel. Poke the flour down with a chopstick. Keep adding flour until the balloon is filled to fist size.

3 Tie the neck of the balloon
in a tight knot. If it is hard
to tie, ask an adult to help you.

4 Cut out pieces of colored tape to make
eyes, a nose, and a mouth. Stick them
on the balloon. Do not try to take the tape
off once you stick it on the balloon because
the balloon
may break.

**★ Helpful Hint ★**
Squeeze the shmoo all
you want, but be careful
to keep the shmoo away
from sharp objects or flour
will fly everywhere!

# Mug Mats

**Weaving is easy and fun —
especially when you get creative!**

**1** Measure ⅓ inch (1 cm) from each short side of the cardboard and make a row of dots ⅓ inch (1 cm) apart. Cut out a triangle-shaped notch at each dot (as shown). You just made a loom!

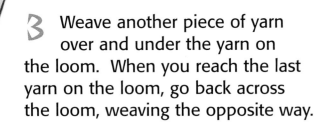

**2** Tie a piece of yarn to a corner of the loom. Wind the yarn up and down over the front of the loom, between the notches, then tie the yarn to the opposite corner.

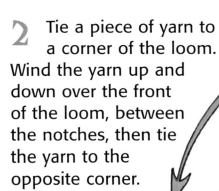

**3** Weave another piece of yarn over and under the yarn on the loom. When you reach the last yarn on the loom, go back across the loom, weaving the opposite way.

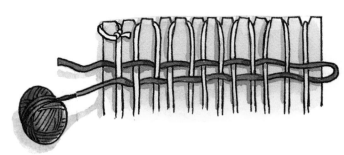

18

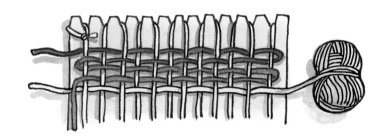

4  To change colors, lay the end of the old color of yarn alongside the yarn on the loom at the end of a row. Weave the end into the mat as you go.

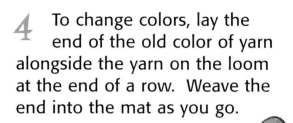

5  Keep weaving until you have a square mat. To take the mat off the loom, cut the loops of yarn around the notches on the loom. Tie together the ends of each loop. With a needle, thread any loose ends into the mat.

★ **Bright Idea** ★

**Change the color of yarn with every row you weave to make stripes. To make big stripes, weave several rows in one color, then change colors.**

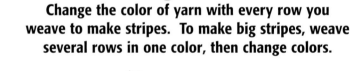

# Swish Dish

**You can use any bowl as a mold to make pretty papier-mâché.**

You Will Need
- two bowls
- petroleum jelly
- white glue
- newspaper
- paintbrush
- pencil and scissors
- white paint
- colored tissue paper
- clear varnish

1 Wipe petroleum jelly over the outside of the bowl you are using as a mold.

2 Mix equal amounts of white glue and water in another bowl.

3 Tear newspaper into strips. Lay each strip onto the mold and brush the glue mixture over it. Overlap the strips as you go. Cover the mold with ten or more layers of paper strips, then let the newspaper dry for several days.

4 Take your new papier-mâché bowl off its mold. Draw a line around the rim of the bowl and trim along the line with scissors.

5 Cover the bowl's rim with newspaper strips dipped in the glue mixture. When the bowl is dry, paint it white. Let the paint dry. Then tear tissue paper into squares.

6 Brush glue onto the bowl and cover the bowl with the paper squares. When the glue is dry, brush on clear varnish.

★ **Helpful Hint** ★
**This bowl can be used for lots of things – but not for liquids!**

# Pencil Pouch

**Let this clever case carry your friend's favorite colored pencils.**

You Will Need
- scissors
- ruler
- strong fabric
- ribbons
- fabric glue
- pencil
- needle
- embroidery floss
- Velcro tape

1 Cut a 10-inch (25-cm) square piece of strong fabric.

2 Cut pieces of colored ribbons shorter than 10 inches (25 cm). Arrange them on one half of the fabric, then glue them in place with fabric glue. Let the glue dry.

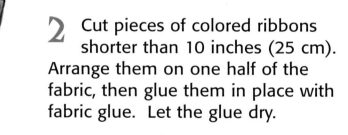

3 Draw a triangle at one end of each ribbon. Thread a needle with embroidery floss. Starting near the ribbon, fill in each triangle with several long stitches. Stitch the tip of each triangle with black floss.

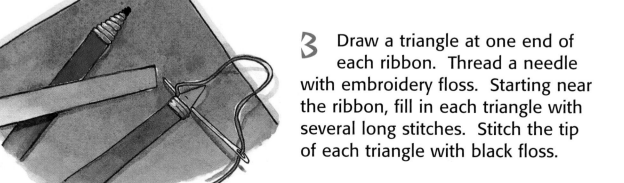

4 Fold the fabric in half to make a pocket, with the ribbons on the inside. In small stitches close to the edge of the fabric, sew the sides of the pocket together. Then turn the pocket ribbon-side out.

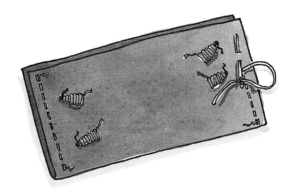

5 Now you have a case. Along the opening of the case, fold in the fabric 1/3 inch (1 cm). Cut a piece of Velcro tape 8 inches (21 cm) long. Use the two sections of the Velcro to tape the folds down inside the case.

★ **Bright Idea** ★
**If you don't have Velcro, ask an adult to help you sew a zipper on your pencil case.**

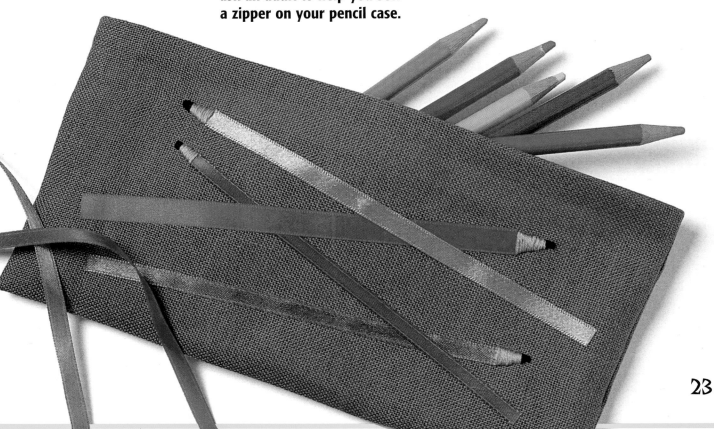

# Hot Pot Hot Pad

**A helpful hot pad is better than dessert for any cook.**

You Will Need

- scissors and ruler
- fabric
- plate
- chalk
- heat-resistant batting for quilting
- straight pins
- needle
- embroidery floss
- wide bias tape

1 Cut fabric into two 8-inch (20-cm) squares. Lay a plate slightly smaller than the squares on one fabric piece. Use chalk to trace a circle around the plate. Draw a simple design in the circle.

2 Cut an 8-inch (20-cm) square of batting. Pin together the two fabric pieces, with the batting in between like a sandwich. With a needle and embroidery floss, sew around the circle, through all three layers.

3 Now use the needle and embroidery floss to sew along the lines of your design in small stitches.

4 Cut out the circle close to its edge. Fold bias tape around the sides of the circle and pin the tape in place. Sew on the tape. Make sure you stitch through all the layers of your circle sandwich.

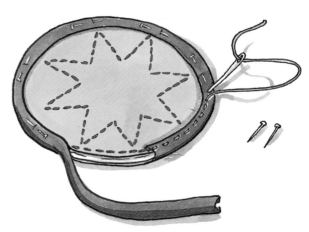

5 Twist the end of the bias tape to make a loop. Stitch around the loop and sew the end of the loop onto the circle. Cut off any extra tape.

★ **Helpful Hint** ★
**Ask an adult to help you
with the stitching**

# Mark My Words

**Fancy tassels on these bookmarks will help anyone find the right page.**

1 Cut out a 1½-inch (4-cm) square of cardboard. Wind embroidery floss around it twenty-five times.

2 Pull a short piece of embroidery floss under the loops of wound floss and tie it in a knot. Slip the loops off the cardboard.

3 Near the tied end of the loops, wind another piece of floss around the loops and tie it in a knot. Cut the bottoms of the loops. You just made a tassel.

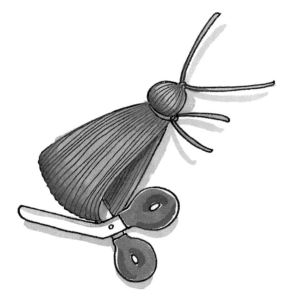

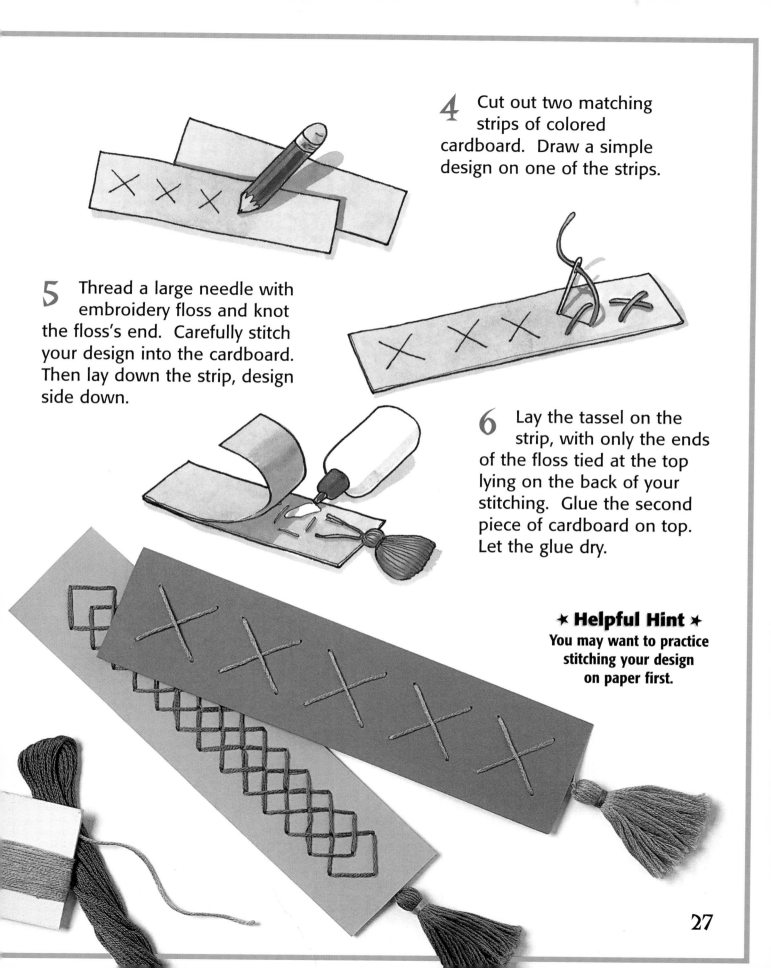

**4** Cut out two matching strips of colored cardboard. Draw a simple design on one of the strips.

**5** Thread a large needle with embroidery floss and knot the floss's end. Carefully stitch your design into the cardboard. Then lay down the strip, design side down.

**6** Lay the tassel on the strip, with only the ends of the floss tied at the top lying on the back of your stitching. Glue the second piece of cardboard on top. Let the glue dry.

★ **Helpful Hint** ★
You may want to practice stitching your design on paper first.

# Bloomers

**A beautiful bouquet makes a gorgeous gift — and this bouquet will last a long time.**

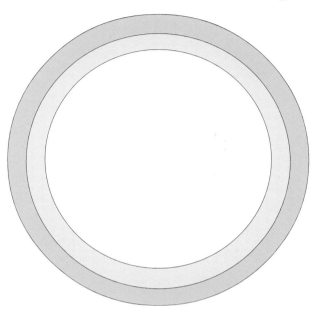

```
You Will Need
• pencil
• tissue paper
• scissors
• straight pins
• paintbrush
• green paint
• wooden skewers
• clear tape
```

1   Trace the three circles above on tissue paper, using a different color of paper for each circle.  Cut the circles out.  You will need three circles for each flower.

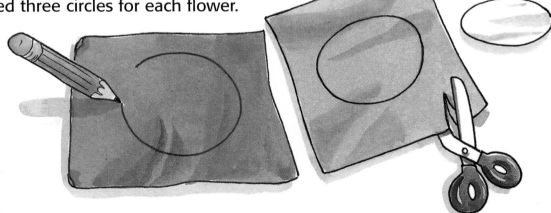

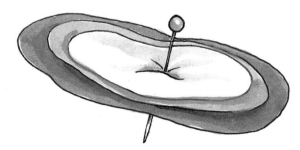

2   Stack the three tissue paper circles, with the smallest circle on top and the largest on the bottom.  Carefully push a pin through the center of the stack.

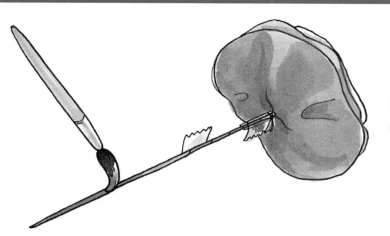

3   Paint a wooden skewer green. Tape the pin lengthwise along the end of the skewer (as shown).

4   To shape the flower, hold the paper circles in one hand while you wind tape loosely around the skewer.

★ **Bright Idea** ★
**To make petals, snip into the circles toward their centers.**

# Take Note!

**Everyone needs
a neat notepad.**

1  Cut a rectangle out
   of colored cardboard.
Cut out a slightly
smaller rectangle
in another color
of cardboard.

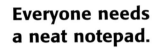

2  Ask an adult to run
   a craft knife lightly
across the middle of
each rectangle.

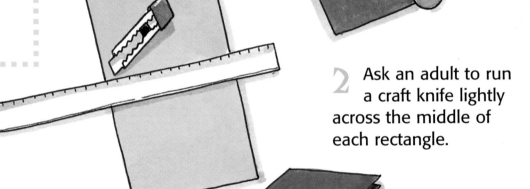

3  Fold the rectangles in half
   along the cuts.  On one
half of the smaller rectangle,
draw a design.  Then
cut out the design.

4   Cut eight pieces of paper the same size as the smaller rectangle of cardboard. Fold all of the paper in half. Stack the cardboard pieces and paper, with the smallest cardboard piece on the bottom and the paper on top.

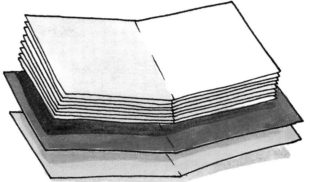

5   Thread a needle. Poke the needle through the fold in the stack, close to one side. Be sure to go through all the stack's layers. Hold onto the end of the thread while you stitch back through the stack, along the fold, and close to the other side. Tie the ends of the thread in a bow.

★ **Bright Idea** ★
Cut your friend's initials into the front of the book to make a personalized present.

31

# A Frame-up

**Noodles come in many amazing shapes — and they make great decorations.**

**You Will Need**
- small mirror
- stiff cardboard
- ruler
- pencil
- craft knife
- paintbrush
- acrylic paints
- strong tape
- noodle shapes
- white glue

1 Place the mirror on cardboard. Draw a rectangle around it 1 inch (3 cm) from its sides. Remove the mirror and draw another rectangle inside the first, 1 ½ inches (4 cm) from the sides of the first. Ask an adult to cut out the rectangles with a craft knife.

2 Now you have a frame. Paint the frame a bright color, then let the paint dry.

3 Use strong tape to tape the mirror onto the back of the frame.

32

4 Paint noodle shapes fun colors, then let the paint dry. Be careful — painting noodles is messy.

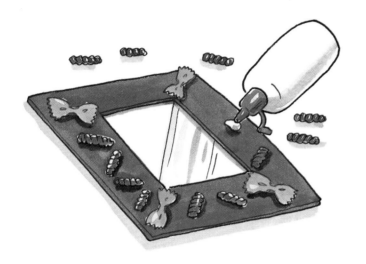

5 Arrange the noodles on the frame, then glue each noodle in place. Let the glue dry.

★ **Bright Idea** ★
To hang the mirror, tape a piece of string onto the back of the frame.

# String Thing

**String can unravel anywhere, but this holder will keep a handle on it.**

### You Will Need
- margarine tub and lid
- paintbrush
- poster paints
- pencil and paper
- scissors
- colored cardboard
- white glue
- large needle
- ball of string

**1** Make sure the margarine tub is clean. Paint the outside of the tub, then let the paint dry.

**2** On scrap paper, design a picture or pattern to fit on the bottom of the tub. Cut out the shapes you need for your picture in colored cardboard, then glue the shapes onto the tub.

**3** Ask an adult to punch a hole through the bottom of the tub with a large needle. Place a ball of string in the tub and pull the end of the string through the hole.

**4** Put the lid on the tub. Ask an adult to punch a hole though the tub's rim and lid with a needle. Pull a short piece of string through this hole, then tie the string in a loop. Use this loop to hang the tub.

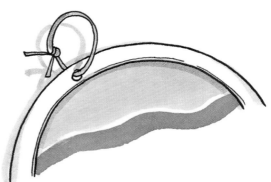

★ **Bright Idea** ★
You can also design a
mouse or a monkey, using
the string for a tail.

35

# Stick 'Em Up

**Make herds of magnetic creatures out of simple salt dough.**

1 Mix flour and salt in a bowl. Add water, a little at a time, and mix until you have a soft dough. Knead the dough with your hands until it is smooth.

### ★ Bright Idea ★
Use cardboard shapes instead of cookie cutters. Lay the shapes on the dough, then cut the dough around them with a dull knife.

2 Ask an adult to preheat the oven to 350° Fahrenheit (180° Celsius). Roll out the dough until it is ⅕ inch (5 mm) thick. Use cookie cutters to cut out fun shapes in the dough.

3 Gently place the shapes on a cookie sheet. Ask an adult to bake them for 2 hours.

4 Let the shapes cool, then paint them bright colors. When the paint is dry, brush clear varnish over the shapes.

5 Glue a small magnet to the back of each shape.

# Mouse Madness

**Your favorite drawing can bring a mousy mouse pad to life.**

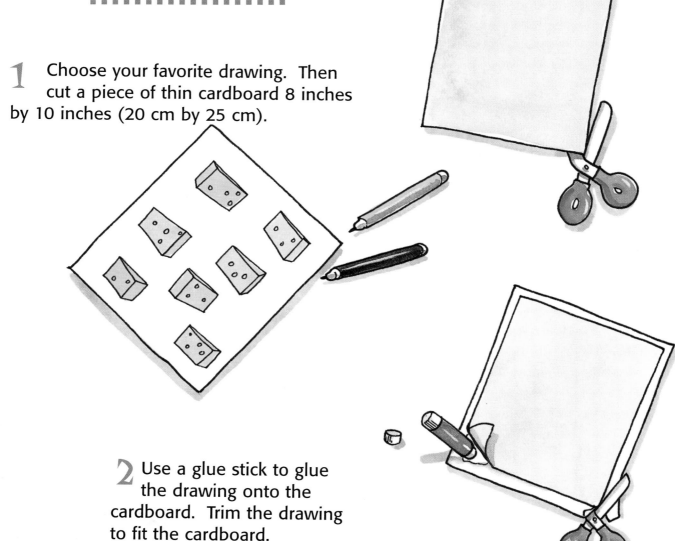

1 Choose your favorite drawing.  Then cut a piece of thin cardboard 8 inches by 10 inches (20 cm by 25 cm).

2 Use a glue stick to glue the drawing onto the cardboard.  Trim the drawing to fit the cardboard.

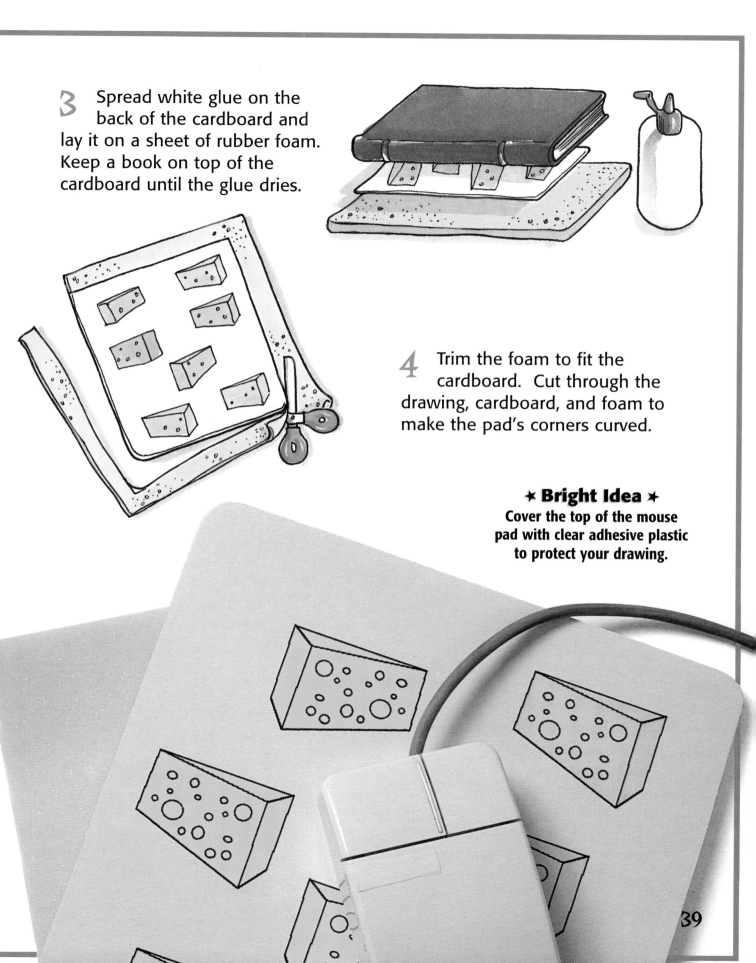

3 Spread white glue on the back of the cardboard and lay it on a sheet of rubber foam. Keep a book on top of the cardboard until the glue dries.

4 Trim the foam to fit the cardboard. Cut through the drawing, cardboard, and foam to make the pad's corners curved.

**★ Bright Idea ★**
Cover the top of the mouse pad with clear adhesive plastic to protect your drawing.

39

# Bath Buddy

**Everyone will enjoy a cuddly bath mitt with a friendly face.**

1 Cut a piece of paper 10 inches by 6 inches (25 cm by 15 cm). Cut curved corners on one short side.

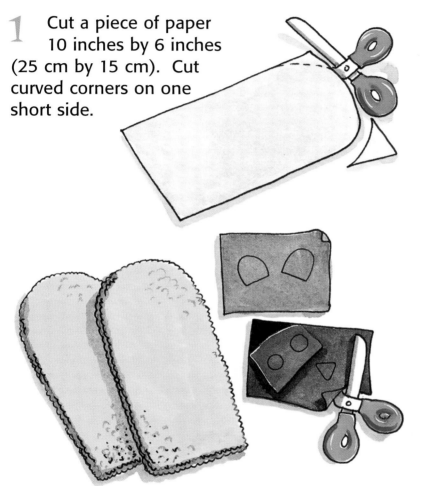

2 Using the paper as a guide, cut two pieces of terry cloth the same size and shape as the paper. On different colors of felt, draw shapes to make ears, eyes, and a nose for your creature, then cut out the shapes.

3 Using a needle and thread, sew the ears onto one piece of cloth by stitching along the bottoms of the ears. Then fold the ears back and sew a single stitch through each ear to hold it in place.

**4** Sew on the eyes with two stitches in the shape of an **X**. Sew the nose on with three stitches that make a triangle. Sew long stitches in the cloth to make a smiling mouth.

**5** Lay the second piece of cloth over the face. Sew the two pieces of cloth together by stitching around the sides 1/3 inch (1 cm) from the edges — but don't sew along the straight side. Now you have a mitt.

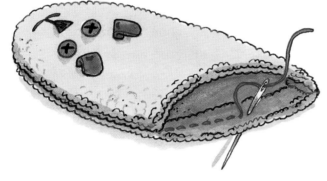

**6** Turn the mitt right side out. Along the open side, fold the cloth inward and sew down the fold inside the mitt.

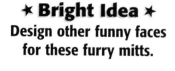

**★ Bright Idea ★**
Design other funny faces
for these furry mitts.

# Killer Key Rings

**These creepy key ring creatures will spook your friends.**

1 Soften the clay by kneading it with your hands. Roll a piece of clay into a ball, then flatten it into a circle.

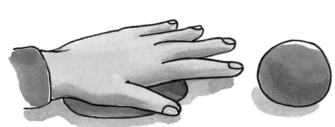

2 Shape small pieces of colored clay into eyes and other details. Press the pieces onto the circle and make a scary monster face.

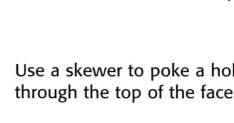

3 Use a skewer to poke a hole through the top of the face.

**4** Place the clay face on a cookie sheet. Ask an adult to bake the clay according to the instructions on the clay's package.

**5** Let the clay face cool and harden. Thread a piece of string through the hole in the face and then through a key ring. Tie the string in a knot. Trim the ends of the string.

★ **Helpful Hint** ★
Use a skewer or a fork to carve into the clay.

# Foxy Boxes

A beautiful box can hold
a present — or be the
present itself.

You Will Need
- old box with a lid
- paintbrush
- paints
- foil candy wrappers
  or aluminum foil
- clear varnish
- white glue
- toothpick

1  Paint a box and
its lid white to
cover up any labels.
When the white paint
is dry, paint the box
a bright color.

2  Carefully flatten foil
candy wrappers or
small squares of aluminum
foil.  Brush clear varnish
over the box.

**3** Scrunch the small pieces of foil into balls or fold them to make diamond shapes. Twist long strips of foil to make silver wires.

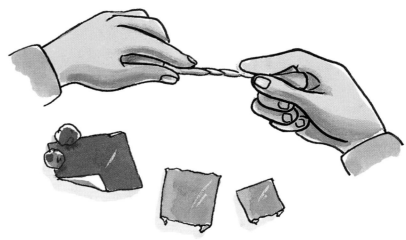

**4** Arrange the foil shapes on the box to create an interesting design. Use a toothpick to spread glue on the shapes and glue them in place. Let the glue dry.

**★ Helpful Hint ★**
Decorate the box's lid first, but don't forget the sides.

45

# It's a Wrap!

**Creative wrapping paper can add a fancy touch to any gift! Here are some ideas on how to make great gift wrap.**

Dip a toothbrush into paint. Hold the toothbrush over plain paper, then brush your finger over it to spatter paint onto the paper.

Use a black marker to draw lots of small designs on white paper. First wrap a gift in the paper, then wrap the gift in a sheet of colored cellophane.

46

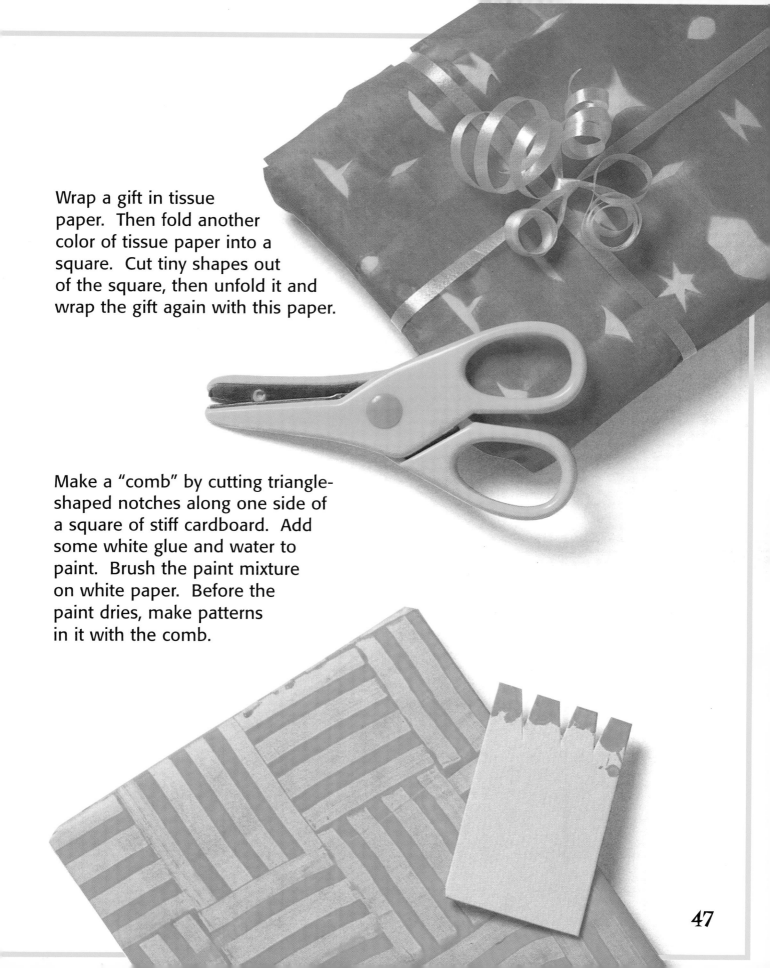

Wrap a gift in tissue paper. Then fold another color of tissue paper into a square. Cut tiny shapes out of the square, then unfold it and wrap the gift again with this paper.

Make a "comb" by cutting triangle-shaped notches along one side of a square of stiff cardboard. Add some white glue and water to paint. Brush the paint mixture on white paper. Before the paint dries, make patterns in it with the comb.

47

# Glossary

**batting:** material made of cotton or polyester fibers and used to fill pillows or pad quilts.

**coat:** (n) a layer of paint or varnish.

**cord:** strong string usually made of several strands of thread or yarn.

**embroidery floss:** thick string made of several strands of thread. It is used to stitch designs on fabric.

**heat-resistant:** not easily damaged by heat.

**knead:** to press and squeeze with the hands over and over.

**quilting:** stitching two pieces of material together with padding in between to make a blanket or quilt or to make a quiltlike object.

**rubber foam:** a soft, squishy material for making mouse pads. Craft or fabric stores sell rubber foam.

**skewers:** pointed metal or wooden sticks used to hold meat together while the meat is roasting.

**varnish:** a sticky, paintlike substance spread over a surface to give it a shiny appearance.

**weave:** to create an object by passing yarn, thread, or strips of material over and under one another. The frame on which material is woven is called a **loom**. The material running up and down on the frame is the **warp**. The material running across the frame is the **weft**.

# More Craft Books by Gareth Stevens

*Crafty Juggling. Crafty Kids* (series).
Nick Huckleberry Beak

*Crafty Magic. Crafty Kids* (series).
Nick Huckleberry Beak

*How to Have Fun with Paper. Art Smart* (series).
Christine Smith

*Modeling Dinosaurs. Draw, Model, and Paint* (series). Isidro Sánchez

# Index

aluminum foil 44, 45

balloons 16, 17
batting 24
boxes 44-45

cardboard 4, 8, 10, 11, 14, 15, 18, 26, 27, 30, 31, 32, 34, 36, 38, 39, 47
cards, gift 4-5, 15
cellophane 46
craft knives 4, 10, 30, 32

embroidery floss 10, 11, 22, 24, 26, 27

fabric 22, 23, 24
   felt 4, 12, 13, 40
   terry cloth 40, 41
foil candy wrappers 44, 45
frames 32-33

glitter 6, 7

magnets 36-37
modeling clay 42, 43

napkin rings 10-11
noodles 32, 33
notebooks 30-31

paints 10, 14, 15, 20, 21, 28, 29, 44, 46
   acrylic 6, 8, 9, 32, 33, 36, 37
   poster 34
paper 30, 31, 34, 40
   colored 5, 7
   newspaper 8, 20
   tissue 5, 20, 21, 28, 29, 47
   wrapping 46-47
papier-mâché 8-9, 20-21
pencil cases 22-23
purses 12-13

quilting 24-25

ribbons 4, 22, 23
rocks, painted 6-7
rubber foam 38, 39

salt dough 36-37
skewers 28, 29, 42
stamps 14, 15

tags, gift 4
tassels 26, 27

varnish 6, 7, 8, 9, 14, 15, 20, 21, 36, 37, 44
Velcro 13, 22, 23

weaving 18-19

yarn 18, 19